The Prepared Preschooler

Courtney Moore, MS Ed

The Prepared Preschooler

Copyright © 2021 by Courtney Moore

All rights reserved. No part of this book may be reproduced in any manner whatsoever without written permission except in the case of brief quotations embodied in critical articles and reviews.

First Printing, 2021

Contents

Dedication	1
Chapter 1: Behavior	2
Chapter 3: Motor Development	8
Chapter 4: Adaptive Development	11
Chapter 5: Cognitive Development	17
Chapter 6: Communication Development	23
Chapter 7: Take - Aways	26
About The Author	28

Dedication

For My Love

This book is dedicated to my husband, Scott, who encouraged me to start putting all my years of knowledge down on paper. I love you more every day!

1

Chapter 1: Behavior

Structure and routine help shape your child's behavior and are imperative when working with and raising children. Children thrive on routine and knowing what comes next. Keeping a set routine throughout the day will give your child a sense of power because they know what is happening and what is expected of them. If you give your child a direction (put that away), and you don't follow through to make sure it is completed, you have no credibility with your child. If your child does not follow the direction the first time, you need to physically help your child complete the task. Using hand-over-hand is a great way to get your child to understand what is expected. Three types of behavior modification are incentives, redirection, and time-out.

INCENTIVES

Incentives in my day were called bribes. This is giving a child something desirable in exchange for an action. This can be anything from a fruit snack or a chocolate treat to extra time outside or extra time reading before bed. Incentives work when the child wants what you have. Using incentives is perfectly acceptable, but you can't use them forever. Say you want your child to clean up the toys on the floor. You present the snack bag (that they do not get at any other time during the day for any reason) and explain the IF/THEN scenario. "If you clean up the toys, then you get the snack." You can give one piece for every one toy that is picked up and put away (if necessary), or if the child picks them all up, then they get the whole bag. If the child will pick up the toys for the small bag of snacks, do this two or three more days in a row. On day four, then you offer the child one bite for every two things that are picked up, and so forth. You start stretching the reward out, so the child must do more and will actually get less. Once a child will change his/her behavior, to get something that you have, you need to use that to your advantage. This is a great time to work on potty training, trying new food, cleaning up toys, or anything that may cause your child to tantrum. Keep the snack bag in clear sight of the child, but do not give it to the child if the task has not been completed.

REDIRECTION

Redirection is turning your child's attention off of one thing and onto another. If your child is having a tantrum to get a snack, remove the snack and pull out a book or toy the child wants. When the child stops the tantrum and focuses on the new activity, you have redirected the attention off of one thing onto another. Redirection is useful in many instances. If your child is playing with a toy too roughly, put the toy in 'time-out' and give your child something new. Tell your child the toy was getting too rough and needed time to cool down. Bring the toy back later and demonstrate the appropriate way to play with the toy. Kids need to be taught how to play, and they learn from seeing that modeled for them.

Redirection changes the focus of one behavior onto something else to re-engage your child in an appropriate task. If your child is hitting or pinching give them something to do with their hands other than the negative behavior. Get a stress ball for the child to squeeze or pull out a toy or book to change the focus. Use words like, "No, hands down" or "No, get your ball", instead of, "No hitting. I don't like it when you hit me. Stop it." Say what you want the child to do, not just 'no' or 'stop'. It is good to say no, but then tell the child a replacement behavior. You can't get rid of bad behaviors without replacing that behavior with something more appropriate.

TIME-OUT

Time-out is a tricky subject. Some children respond well to time-out, and some don't care at all if they are put in time-out. Some children won't stay in a time-out area. Then what do you do? Time-out is meant to take the child away from something pleasurable to being absent from it. The child must want to do whatever it is for time-out to be able to effectively change the behavior. If your child doesn't want to be somewhere and throws a tantrum to get you to move them out of that situation, then time-out is not going to be effective. Your child will learn that if they don't like something and throws a tantrum and you take them away from it, then your child got exactly what was wanted. This requires re-thinking on your part.

Time-out should be one minute for every year that child is old, plus one more minute. If your child is 2-years old, then time-out is three minutes. After those three minutes, your child does not remember why they are there and the time-out is useless. After the three minutes are up and before you let your child back to the activity, you need to explain why they were there. For example, "You were in time-out because you hit. Hands down. Can you show me hands down? Great, now you are going to have nice hands and will keep them to yourself. What do you do with your hands? Yes, hands down." Time-out should never continue to the next day or after the child has been removed from the situation. It's over, move on. If time-out doesn't work, use an incentive or redirection.

Chapter 2: Social Development

Social development means how a child interacts with people. How the child plays, shares, asks for help, and uses words to communicate with others indicates how the child is developing socially. Does your child play alone in the presence of other children? Does your child allow other children to play with the same materials? Can your child willingly share toys with others? Does your child make eye contact with others when someone is speaking to them? It may not seem like a big deal, but how your child interacts with others socially is a big indicator of how your child is developing. If this is not happening, your child may not be developing typically and may need some professional evaluations to determine if early intervention is needed. Your child's social skills may vary depending on whether they are interacting with family or others in the community. This is typical and a good thing. You want your child to be initially uneasy around strangers until you say it is o.k. to go play.

FAMILY SOCIALIZATION

When a child is at home with family members, it is important to see how the child interacts with those around them. Encourage family activities that do not include electronic devices (TV, iPad, gaming, etc.) Social development is not an innate skill, meaning a child does not automatically know how to play appropriately with others. You need to model how to play. Sit on the floor and build with blocks or Legos. You put two together, then hand your child two blocks to put together. If your child does not put the blocks together, put your hands over your child's hands, and do it with them. Do NOT do it for your child. Your child needs to feel the motor movements of how to do the action.

When a child is playing alone in a room, walk over and engage the child in play. Get down on the child's level, even if it means sitting on the floor or pulling up a chair so you are more at eye level with your child. Use the words "my turn, your turn" to initiate social play. It is important to establish eye contact with your child because, in a social world, people expect to be looked at during conversations. If your child does not make eye contact when you call his/her name, use your hand to gently guide the child's chin towards you to make eye contact. If your child does not look at you when you call his/her name, get within 2 feet, and call the name again. If the child still does not look at you, move within arms' reach and call the child's name and help guide the chin to look at you when you call the name. If the child does make eye contact, praise, praise, praise. Be overdramatic, happy.

Dos and Don'ts to help your child learn appropriate social skills.

DO NOT: Let your child play alone on the tablet, phone, gaming system, YouTube, or watch television for hours on end. (I understand needing to use a device while you catch a much-needed shower, or take care of bills, but no more than 30 minutes at a time.)

Do: Set a timer for yourself if you need to, to make sure you don't lose track of time.

DO NOT: Call your child's name 3, 5, 10, 20 times without a response. Every time you call your child's name, over and over again, your child's brain has to reprocess what you said.

DO: Give your child a direction, wait 5-10 seconds for your child to process what you said. If you give a direction and give it again in 3 seconds, and again in 3 more seconds your child's brain resets every time, so that child has not had the chance to understand what you are asking. Some children need more processing time. It is o.k. to wait a few seconds to see if your child can follow a one-step direction. If you need to count to 10 in your head after you give your child a direction, then do that. It will give you an idea of how long your child needs to process what you have said. If your child does not follow through with what you asked after 10 seconds, give the child the direction again then take the child's hands and lead them through the activity you asked to be done. If you don't show your child what you want your child may not understand what you want to happen.

COMMUNITY SOCIALIZATION

Socialization is critical to the overall development of a child. Children learn communication and social skills more through interaction with their peers in the community than through any other means. Teaching your child how to interact appropriately with other children, ones who are not family members (cousins, siblings, etc), will take time and practice. Children need to have good social interaction modeled for them. Turn-taking, sharing, conflict resolution, and using language to initiate communication are all part of learning social skills. It can be difficult at the local park to find children to effectively teach social skills, but not introducing that to children can cause detrimental effects. If/When conflicts arise amongst children, it is important to talk through how to resolve the issue on their own, without requiring adult intervention. "How could you have done that differently", or "Remember, use your words to say my turn", or "You can have a turn when I am done", can help prompt a child to resolve a conflict without any physical aggression.

Chapter 3: Motor Development

Motor skills are broken into 3 areas/subdomains: Gross motor, Fine motor, and Perceptual motor. Gross motor skills involve the large muscles in the body, such as sitting up, crawling, walking, and jumping. Fine motor skills involve the small muscles in the body, such as holding a cup or bottle, using a fork, holding a writing utensil, and buttoning, zipping, and snapping fasteners. Perceptual motor skills involve hand-eye coordination, such as putting pieces in a puzzle, drawing shapes, and stacking blocks. All of these skills combined make up the motor development of a child.

GROSS MOTOR

Gross motor skills are important in the development of a child's ability to move around the environment. Basic skills such as your child holding his/her head up when pulled to sitting from a lying position, to being able to catch a thrown playground ball in later years are examples of Gross motor skills. Movement is important to overall development for your child to gain skills needed in life. Pedaling a tricycle, standing on one foot, walking up and down stairs while alternating feet on each step, and jumping off the floor with both feet together are all skills you as a parent should be helping your child learn. Going to the playground, or taking a walk around the block (with your child walking, not sitting in a wagon the entire way) is a great way to encourage the development of gross motor skills. Performing a simple motor/movement activity not only helps your child's muscle growth, but it can also improve other skills like attending to a task, using words to express what you see, and teaching your child to safely walk with you. Teaching skills like 'walk with me' will help your child stay with you (which is imperative when going shopping or anywhere outside the home). You the parent have to teach your child the skills you want them to know.

Try this...

Play a game as you walk. Tell your child. "Run". Run for about 3 seconds with your child, and then say, "Stop." Make sure you are within arms reach of your child. Help your child stop if they keep going. Tell your child, "Walk with me." Walk for about 3 seconds, then say, "Stop." Again, make sure your child is following the direction as you give it. Repeat with the "run" direction, then walk, etc. Once your child has this down and can follow the direction, switch it up and throw in a different direction like "Hop" or "Jump like a frog." Keep going back to the "walk with me" direction. When your child follows the direction praise, praise, praise your child. You have to teach your child this skill though, your child will not automatically know this. Make it a game.

FINE MOTOR

Fine motor skills are important in the development of a child's ability to use his/her hands to manipulate objects in the environment. Basic skills include dropping an object intentionally when shown how, taking toddler wooden puzzle pieces out of the board, or buttoning, snapping snaps or zipping a zipper. Picking up a small object like a Lego or even a Cheerio and placing it in a cup, and scribbling on paper are examples of fine motor tasks.

You can help your child learn these tasks by making learning fun. Practice picking up items one at a time, first by saying, "My turn", and then you pick up a small item. Next, have your child use his/her fingers to pick up an item when you say, "Your turn". Go back and forth until all items are picked up. When your child completes the task, praise, praise, praise. "Great job, what a helper, good job picking up the toys when I asked." Try to name the thing in which you are praising your child, so your child understands what they did to get the praise.

PERCEPTUAL MOTOR

Perceptual motor skills are important in the development of a child's ability to use hand-eye coordination. Play a game with your child. Your child should be able to stack one-inch blocks or big interlocking blocks one at a time. You can help show your child how to push the Legos together to make them 'stick'. Count the blocks as they are stacked. Name the colors as your child picks them up. Have your child repeat the number or color. Practice dropping buttons into a butter tub with a slit cut in the middle of it. Let your child take the lid off of the toothpaste or water bottle, and then put it back on again. Practice drawing lines in shaving cream with their pointer finger or draw circles with a crayon or in the soap in the bathtub.

Chapter 4: Adaptive Development

Adaptive skills are those 'self-help' skills or daily living skills that involve taking care of oneself. These daily living skills include feeding skills like using a spoon, drinking from a cup, chewing food and swallowing, and toileting skills like knowing when to use the toilet, managing clothing in the bathroom, and flushing the toilet. You want your child to be as independent as possible, so allow your child the time and opportunity to work on these skills all during the day, especially at mealtime, when teaching toileting skills, and when bathing and dressing.

MEALTIME

Routines are IMPORTANT. Children respond better, just like we do when they know what to expect. This carries over into mealtime. It may sound harsh, but you aren't raising a pet. You shouldn't just leave food around for your child to find and on which to feed whenever they feel like it. Children need structure, and mealtime is no exception. Meals should be eaten at the table, without the TV or tablet. This is your time as a parent to talk to your child. Show your child by your example of how eating at the table should look. You should not be on your phone or involved in a television show either. If your child is just learning to use a spoon (under two years old), you will need to help your child learn how to hold the spoon. You will need to put your hand on top of your child's hand, while your child is holding the spoon, scoop from the bowl, and take the spoon to the mouth.

If your child is just learning to drink from a cup (not a sippy cup, I mean an open-top cup), pour just enough liquid like water, or something that will not stain clothes, into the cup for your child to know there is something in the cup. You don't need to add laundry to your to-do list for the day. Help your child hold the cup, tip it up, and talk through the steps of drinking. Open your mouth a little, tip the cup up slowly and get a little into your mouth, ok, close your mouth and swallow. It takes time and effort. A sippy cup is o.k. in the car or at the babysitter's house, but when you sit at the table for mealtime, practice this skill.

Children aren't born knowing how to properly hold a spoon, or how to scoop, or how to put a spoon into the mouth without dumping the food all over them. Is it messy? Yes! Does it take time and effort on your part? Yes! Do you still want to be hand feeding your child when your child is 10 years old because you never taught them how to feed them? NO! A little effort at an early age will not only free up mealtime for you as a parent but will give your child a sense of accomplishment and pride. When you start backing off your hand-over-hand help and only help your child scoop the food and let your child take the spoon to the mouth independently, that is a great accomplishment. Praise, praise, praise your child. This is a big deal! Plastic bibs that can be laundered or wiped down are wonderful, so don't forget to use them and pack them in your diaper bag.

TOILETING

This may be a difficult subject for some. I have been in a meeting with a parent who said she wasn't going to 'force' her child to use the toilet, or to go to bed. I am not advocating forcing a child to use the toilet, but if you never encourage your child to do anything your child will NEVER do anything. Children typically do not inherently want to do things that are new or difficult. Children will learn to want to do new things if they are praised and encouraged. Toilet training is no different.

Here are some things to take into consideration before getting into the steps of how to toilet train your child.

Signs. Your child should show signs of readiness for toilet training.

- If your child brings you a clean diaper to change a soiled diaper, then your child is ready to be toilet trained.
- If your child will only urinate or defecate when in a pull-up, and not in underwear because they do not like the feel of it in regular underwear, then your child is ready to be toilet trained.
- If your child typically is wet or has a bowel movement around the same time every day, then your child is ready to be toilet trained.
- If your child stays dry for more than a couple of hours at a time while playing around the house, then your child is ready to be toilet trained.
- If your child can take off his/her diaper when it is wet or soiled, then your child is ready to be toilet trained.
- If your child keeps his/her diaper dry, and only wets or soils it when they go off to hide in a corner, then your child is ready to be toilet trained.

Other factors. There are extenuating circumstances that may keep your child from being toilet trained. These factors may include some of the following.

- Your child does not have a consistent routine (same basic schedule during the day.)
- Your child does not have a caregiver who will take the time to follow the toilet training schedule for your child.
- Your child has a physical or medical condition that prevents them from sitting on the toilet.

- Your child does not have the right incentive to be toilet trained. More about that in the Discipline section.
  - Use an incentive to get your child to sit on the toilet and then to use the toilet. If your child likes fruit snacks, show the fruit snack and give it only if something happens.

BATHING/DRESSING

Most parents want their children to be independent as adults. The question is, at what point should you begin letting your child do things alone? Basic skills such as dressing or even bathing can begin as soon as your child shows an understanding of following a one-step direction. A one-year-old who is sitting upright and can raise his/her arms can help get dressed. Put a shirt over your child's head and have your child put his/her arms in the arm-holes independently. Set your child on the floor and have the child step into elastic waist pants and pull the pants up by themselves. When you are potty training have your child pull his/her pants up when getting off the toilet. It's ok to wait 10 seconds with the pants down around the ankles to see if your child recognizes the need to pull up the pants. If your child does not attempt to pull up the pants, then you can reach around, put your hands on top of your child's hands and go through the motions of pulling up the pants. You may be amazed at how quickly your child can pick up that skill.

Bath time is also a great time to start talking about body parts. When washing your child in the bathtub, name each body part as you wash. "I'm going to wash your face, scrub, scrub, can you wash your face now?" Face, head, arms, hands, legs, feet, stomach, back. Once you have washed all the parts, make a game of it, and give the washrag to your child. "Now it's your turn, wash your _____ (insert a body part name)." If your child does it correctly praise, praise, praise. "Great job, you washed your _____. Let's try another. Can you wash your _____?"

If your child is not able to wash the part you named, then point to the correct body part on your child and say, 'this is your _____, can you wash your _____ (same body part again)?" Your child should be able to follow your direction. Keep doing this until your child can correctly identify each of the basic body parts by touching/washing them. The next step is for you to point to one of those body parts and see if your child can name that body part. "Time to wash this part (point to a body part), what is this one called?" If your child does not answer, then say the body part name. "This is your _____ (name part)." Then ask your child again, "what is this called?" Once the basic parts are understood and able to be named by your child, then add new body parts (shoulder, elbow, chest, ankle, chin, etc.)

A child learns by repetition and through play, so make it a game and give your child a chance to be successful. You can play the body parts game with a small stuffed animal or a small piece of clothing like a sock. "Let's be silly. "Put the sock on your head, put it on your leg, put it on your foot." Every interaction is a chance to teach your child, and kids love to be praised. When the child has that concept, start mislabeling your body parts to see if your child recognizes play. Put the toy on your leg and say, "Is the toy on my head?" Wait for your child to respond. If your child does not respond, answer your question. "No, the toy isn't on my head; it is on my leg. Can you put it on your leg? Silly mommy/daddy, let's try that again." Move it around to get your child to see and recognize correct names for body parts, and to start being able to answer "yes/no" correctly. Always give your child the correct answer if they do not respond, or if they respond incorrectly.

Dressing skills also develop through repetition. Start by putting your child's shirt over the head, and have your child put his/her arms through the armholes. You can help guide the arms the first few times until your child gets the hang of it. For pants, have your child sit and put his/her feet in the pants and have your child stand up and pull the pants up the rest of the way. I talked about this in toilet training also. For coats or sweaters, hold the item up so your child can put in their arms. Start the zipper and have your child pull the zipper up independently. Your child should also be able to unzip a coat, even if it is only to the bottom but cannot yet be pulled apart. Every step you teach your child to do independently is one more action that you as a parent do not have to do. We have enough other responsibilities that our child cannot do, so encourage your child to do what they can!

Chapter 5: Cognitive Development

Cognitive skills are those things that involve memory, critical thinking, reasoning, language, abstract concepts, literacy, etc. These skills altogether are what we refer to as a DQ or developmental quotient. Your child's cognitive skills develop through what they see, experience, do, hear, and in what they participate. You may have heard the phrase, "a child is like a sponge, and always absorbing what is around him." This is so true, so giving your child as many opportunities to learn and participate in life is the best way to help your child's cognitive growth. Let's touch on a few easy ways to increase your child's cognitive abilities.

COLORS (MATCHING, POINTING, NAMING)

Matching colors is the first and easiest step. A child will learn to match what is seen before starting to point to a named color, or finally naming colors correctly. Use color words when talking about objects in daily life. Instead of saying, "bring me the truck," say, "bring me the blue truck" or whatever the color of the truck may be. Using descriptive words (like color words) will increase your child's cognitive/thinking skills and will increase your child's language. Matching by color is easy. After breakfast, given a bowl of dry fruit-loops, have your child pull out all the _____ (insert color) ones and put them in a bowl. You put a few of one color in the bowl and ask your child to do this. Just start with one color. When your child can do this successfully (every day for 5 days or so), then have your child pick out two colors that you choose. Always give your child a model (you do it first and leave those in the bowl so your child can match them.)

When your child has finished matching colors, let them eat them as a reward, but not until you are done matching. Delay the gratification. You can do this activity with fruit snacks, cereal, colored goldfish, etc. Once you think your child has the concept, then expand the matching to blocks or same color cars, or whatever things of which you have multiples. Once your child can match colors, then you can move on to the next step.

Pointing to colors when named is the skill that comes after matching colors. Make it easy at first. Give your child all one color of an item. "Touch yellow." This should be easy because all of the items are yellow. Praise, praise, praise, by saying, "Yes, you touched yellow". Repeat that for several days, and then switch up the color. The second week, try that with red. Give your child all red objects. Have your child give you red and say the color as they point to or hand you the red ones. "Good job, you touched red, can you show me something else that is red? Great!"

When you think your child has that down, then give your child the two colors on which you have worked. Ask your child, "Touch the red one." If your child does that, switch the placement of the two objects and ask for red again. It is important to see if your child always picks the one on the right side/ or left side, or if your child understands the concept of red or yellow. Add new colors as your child masters the previous colors. Now you are ready to move on to naming colors.

Naming colors is the last in the process of identifying colors. This is the most difficult, as your child has to see what you are presenting, process what you are saying, and find and use language to complete the task. Most children will pick a "color word", and everything becomes that color to them for a while, even when it is not. Yellow seems to be a particularly common color that kids name for every color. This will pass, as you practice matching and pointing to a named color, but don't be surprised if this happens for a while. Don't give up on naming colors.

When talking with your child, make sure you are using color words when describing objects. "I have on a purple shirt today, what color is your shirt?" The more you expose your child to words that describe things the broader your child's concept of language will grow. When your child says a color word try and link it to something in the world that will bring up a visual image. For instance, when saying 'yellow', use a phrase like "yellow like the sun" or "yellow like a banana." Other comparisons could include: green like grass, blue like the ocean or the sky, orange like a pumpkin, red like an apple, etc. Use things that your child has seen and can relate to. If your car is blue, then use "blue like mommy's car." Make colors meaningful to your child.

When learning color names, it is ok to give your child a 'hint' by giving the first sound of the word. So instead of telling your child the color is red when you ask if your child doesn't answer, or answers incorrectly, make the "R" sound and see if your child can finish the word. Once your child can do that, back off on giving the sound. Naming colors is the final step in the cognitive process for color recognition so do the steps in order and your child will be more successful.

NUMBERS (COUNTING)

Numbers and counting are skills that can be learned at an early age and can be done anywhere with anything. The concept of one-to-one correspondence means being about to hear a number and correctly identify that many of something. For example, if I say the number 2, I would expect you to count out 1, 2 items, and give me both of them. Numbers and counting are all around us and can be taught easily. If your child is having a snack, only give them one chip. When your child eats that one and looks at you like you have lost your mind by only giving one, ask your child "how many more do you want, one or two?" If your child responds with a number, count that number out and put it on the plate (even if that number is more than 1 or 2.) This will teach your child that numbers have meaning, and they can get more if they give a bigger number.

Count the toys as your child is putting them away in the toy box, count shoes as you ask your child to go get his/her shoes so you both can go outside to play. Count cars as you drive by them. Use your words, so your child learns to use his/her words. Use phrases like, "I see 3 cars," or "I need two shoes." You may feel silly talking seemingly to yourself throughout the day, but your child is listening and will learn as you describe what you are doing.

SORTING (GROUPING)

Sorting is different from matching, in that the child has to understand similarities and differences in objects. Sorting can be by size, color, shape, use, or category. In the classroom, we start with sorting by color, which is the easiest skill, first. To sort by color, your child needs to be able to identify colors. That makes sense, right? If you say, 'give me all the red fruit loops', your child has to have previous knowledge of what the color red is, and then be able to determine which of the items are red and which are not. Typically, if you hold out your hand and ask a preschooler for all the red objects, as long as your hand is extended, the child will continue to put items in your hand regardless of the color. This is the first step in learning how to sort.

Sorting with demonstration, meaning you do it first, then mix the colors up and have your child imitate that skill is teaching the art of sorting. This is a big step if your child can complete that task by watching you do it. Next, you mix the colors and ask for a different color without showing your child what you mean first. If your child can do this, then it is time to move on to a higher level-thinking task.

Next, you sort by shape, but your child needs to be able to tell the difference between a circle, square, triangle, and then by size, meaning big or little. After your child can do this, then you start adding a second attribute. "Give me all the big, red blocks," or "give me all the little, green blocks." Finally, you work your child into the ability to sort by 3 attributes at once meaning by size, shape, and color. After this is accomplished you can move on to sorting by category. Putting things in categories means asking for all the things with wheels (transportation), or all the fruit, or all the clothes you wear in the summer. The list is endless and can be used to expand your child's understanding that things can be grouped into categories and sorted accordingly.

LABELING (NAMING)

Labeling or naming objects is both language/communication and a cognitive skill also. You want your child to be able to tell you what they want, so you name items in your house. Encourage your child to use words to name objects or pictures in a book. Sit and look at a book with your child sitting in your lap. You don't have to read every word on every page every time. Reading is essential to language, but having your child point to pictures in a book is also important. "I see the sun, do you see the sun? Touch the picture of the sun. Great job!!!!" Labeling objects gives your child the words to be able to ask for what they want, and greatly reduces tantrums. Don't let your child just lead you to the kitchen and point to the refrigerator and scream. That only teaches your child that you are a good guesser. If you know what your child wants, take the item and hold it, say the name of the object, then ask your child to say the name of the object. Labeling objects is how we learn to ask for what we want.

LITERACY (READING)

Literacy is a HUGE learning area for your child. So many new words, concepts, places, and language skills are incorporated into literacy. Reading to your child is essential to your child's future educational success. Reading a book is not just learning you're A, B, Cs, and sounding out words. Literacy involves critical thinking skills (cognitive), attention (adaptive skills), being able to sit for a story (social/adaptive), identifying pictures (language), and turning pages (fine motor), just for starters. Pick a book that has good pictures, short sentences, may rhyme and your child can help turn the pages. My kid's favorite books growing up were "The Foot Book" by Dr. Seuss, and "Goodnight Moon" by Margaret Wise Brown. Pick any book you like, but read to your child. When your child starts to use words, read part of the sentence from the book, and stop and let your child fill in the missing words. Read, read, read.

Chapter 6: Communication Development

Communication does not mean verbally talking; it means being able to let someone else know what you think, want, or need. I have heard so many parents say, "I don't want my child to learn to sign because I want them to talk." Do you want your child to keep having tantrums because they are frustrated? Do you want to keep your child from expressing themselves? Do you think people who are deaf and using sign language are not 'talking' to each other because they aren't using their voice? Communication is the ability to let others know what is on your mind.

In the classroom, we use basic sign language, pictures, true objects, and verbal language to communicate. I want my preschoolers to communicate, not necessarily to 'talk.' Think about this. If your child can use verbal language, encourage verbal language, but if your child has never said a word, don't you want that child to have some form of communication? Motor skills develop before verbal language skills, so it only makes sense to use sign language or pointing to pictures while your child's verbal skills develop. Some children can understand more than they say, and that is the difference between receptive and expressive language.

RECEPTIVE LANGUAGE

Receptive language refers to the ability of one to understand language. Children can have higher receptive language, and lower expressive language. The trick is, to use that receptive (understanding) skill to your advantage to elicit the expressive (verbal) skill. Receptive skills may look like a child being able to follow a one-step direction, such as "go get your shoes", or "put that in the trash." If your child can follow a routine direction, point to something you name, or get and bring back to you something you name, then your child has good receptive skills. It is age-appropriate if your child can hear a statement or direction from you, understand what you say, and complete the simple task.

If your child is not able to follow a routine direction or go get a cup or shoes then practice is needed to teach your child how to do these things. Receptive skills generally develop earlier than expressive skills. To start helping your child, pick one skill that you want them to do. Something easy. Start with "give it to me", or "get your cup/shoes/toy." Get your child's attention (remove any distractions – turn off the TV, take away the tablet, etc.), use short and simple phrases.

EXPRESSIVE

Expressive language refers to the ability to say (talk) words. Children who have good receptive skills may need extra encouragement to use their expressive words. If your child can follow simple directions and find objects you name, but not able to name objects or tell you what they want, then your child needs help with expressive language. Sometimes, children don't use expressive language, because they don't need to use it. If a child can get what they want, without using any words, where is the incentive to use words? There is no need to use words because mom or dad, or grandma know exactly what the child likes to eat, drink, or play with and puts it all in reach of the child.

To get a child to start to use words expressively, you must make it difficult for them. Sometimes we use the term 'sabotage' to explain what we mean. If your child can grab a cup, and shake it at you, and you automatically fill the cup, the child does not need to use verbal language. But, if you move the cup so the child can't reach it when the child takes you into the kitchen, the ball (or cup) is in your court.

Hold up two choices from the kitchen, the cup, and a snack. Ask the child what do they want? Don't let the child grab either item. Ask the child to point to which one is wanted. If it is the cup, say, "Oh, you want the cup?" Make the hard C sound, c-c-c, and ask the child to try the sound. "You try it, C-C-C." If they make any attempt at the sounds, fill the cup and hand it over. Praise, praise, praise. If the child does not make any sound, withhold the cup then try again. (Note, the tantrums will get worse before they get better the first few days you try this technique. Just remember, as long as your child isn't endangering themselves, a tantrum isn't the end of the world.) If a tantrum occurs because the child didn't make the sound, put the cup away, and walk away. When the child has calmed down, take them back into the kitchen and repeat the steps of saying the word cup.

If you give in easily, there is no reason for your child to NEED to speak. Once you start to get the initial sound from the child, then add the rest of the sounds to produce the whole word. Once this works with the cup, choose a second item (snack), and work on that starting with the initial sound. Use an item that is highly liked by your child. This will work, but you have to be consistent and not give in. I would recommend starting this during the daytime, not at mealtime, since you want your child to stay interested. You can sabotage them even more by giving them a salty snack, so you know they are thirsty and there is more motivation to get the cup.

Chapter 7: Take - Aways

Having young children requires work. Lots of work. Some children are more challenging than others. This is when you must look for other resources to help you. I learn new tips and techniques every year from other parents, educational classes, and just life. Don't be afraid to ask for help. There is no perfect book on how to parent, but there are resources out there to help you. Every parent has wonderful days and days that make us want to lock the door and never come out. The beauty is that you are not the first parent to have a child who behaves a certain way and help is available; you just need to seek it out.

Good parenting is achieved by using all the available resources around you to help your child grow and be independent. Parents want to see their children succeed. Not every parent is willing to put in the time and work to do that.

If you have concerns that your child isn't developing like you think they should, then reach out to your local school system and ask for help. Ask your pediatrician if there is anything atypical about your child's development. It is better to ask and find that everything is ok than to wait until your child is school age and unable to function independently.

If you want more information about child development or tips and tricks, email me at PreparedPreschooler@gmail.com.

About Me:

My name is Courtney Moore. I am an Early Childhood Special Education (ECSE) teacher, and mother of 3 children. I have a bachelor's degree in Early Childhood Psychology, and Early Childhood General education, and a Master's of Science in Education degree in ECSE. The ECSE classroom serves children ages 2 years old through five years old before they enter kindergarten. All of the children in the class have been identified as having some sort of developmental delay or a delay in another area (i.e.: speech, vision, hearing, autism, other health impairment, etc.). I have been an ECSE teacher for 26 years, and I LOVE MY JOB. My job/career has taught me many things over the years, but the biggest thing I have learned is how to help a child develop. Child development entails many aspects: Behavior skills, social skills, motor skills, adaptive skills, cognitive skills, and communication skills. These skills are what makes a child successful or not in life and school.

PARENTING IS HARD. Parenting requires making difficult choices for and with our children, and means sometimes we have to be the 'bad guy' for a minute to get a good result. Parenting requires you to spend one-on-one time with your children, not time with a tablet, watching TV, or playing alone. You are your children's first teacher. You are the one who will set the bar of excellence for your children. If you don't expect greatness, your children will never produce greatness. For those readers who say, but I don't have time, or I'm a single parent, or I don't have the money, my only response is, "What is your priority?" Our children have to be our priority. They are our future. Put time into your children. They deserve it! If you put these skills into practice, you will see a difference if you stick with it.

www.ingramcontent.com/pod-product-compliance
Lightning Source LLC
Chambersburg PA
CBHW071847290426
44109CB00017B/1960